Requirements Elicitation Techniques
Simply Put!

Helping Stakeholders Discover and Define Requirements for IT Projects

Thomas Hathaway
Angela Hathaway

Ordering Information:

Quantity sales. Special discounts are available on quantity purchases by corporations, associations, and others. For details, contact the publisher at books@BusinessAnalysisExperts.com.

The content of this book is also available as an eCourse at http://businessanalysisexperts.com/product/ecourse-requirements-elicitation-techniques-simply-put/

ISBN-10: 1534919228
ISBN-13: 978-1534919228

DEDICATION

This work is dedicated to future generations of Business Analysts, Product Owners, Subject Matter Experts, Domain Experts, COOs, CEOs, Line Managers, and anyone responsible for representing the business community's interests on an Information Technology project.

CONTENTS

ACKNOWLEDGMENTS

This publication would not have been possible without the active support and hard work of our daughter, Penelope Hathaway. We would also be remiss if we did not acknowledge the thousands of students with whom we have had the honor of working over the years. We can honestly say that every single one of you influenced us in no small way.

Finally, we would like to acknowledge Harvey, the fictional Pooka created by Mary Chase and made famous by the movie of the same name with James Stewart. Very early in our marriage we recognized that a third entity is created and lives whenever we work closely on a concept, a new idea, or a new product. Over the years, this entity became so powerful and important to us that we decided to name it Harvey and he should rightfully be listed as the author of this and all of our creative works. Unfortunately, Harvey remains an invisible being, living somewhere beyond our physical senses but real nonetheless. Without Harvey, neither this book nor any of our other publications would have been possible. For us, Harvey embodies the entity that any collaborative effort creates and he is at least as real as each of us. We would truly be lost without him.

PREFACE

Requirement elicitation is the first step in gathering user requirements. It is the process of interacting with all project stakeholders to capture and comprehend their individual and collective business needs. The importance of requirements elicitation cannot be overstated. The requirements you elicit and gather are the foundation for the remainder of ALL of the work on the project.

This book is a continuation of our Requirements Elicitation series. The previously published "Requirements Elicitation Interviews and Workshops – Simply Put" deals with soft skills needed to elicit requirements. This book, "Requirements Elicitation Techniques – Simply Put", is all about specific techniques designed to improve the outcomes of your elicitation interviews and workshops.

The presented techniques will help practicing business analysts, future business analysts, subject matter experts, managers, product owners, project managers, and anyone responsible for getting the right requirements from the right people.

Many people elicit requirements in an organization under the guise of 'business analysis' although it is not in their job description. Whether you are the CEO, COO, Director, Manager, or on the front lines, you may be involved in defining how technology can benefit you and your organization. When you are in that awesome role, you are at that time "the one wearing the Business Analysis (BA) hat".

So what are you going to learn? This book presents some of the nuts and bolts of "requirements elicitation" which will help you:

⇨ Identify potential stakeholders early in the project

⇨ Manage the requirements elicitation process with a Question File

⇨ Recognize, track, and report progress toward requirements completion

⇨ Define, document, and analyze business problems to ferret out hidden requirements

⇨ Facilitate effective requirements brainstorming sessions to uncover additional requirements

⇨ Use 10 critical questions to initiate the requirements elicitation process

⇨ Capture and communicate assumptions about your requirements

⇨ Avoid "analysis paralysis" by recognizing when it is time to stop eliciting and start deciding

You can learn more business analysis techniques by visiting the Business Analysis Learning Store at

(http://businessanalysisexperts.com/business-analysis-training-store/)

to see a wide selection of business analysis books, self-paced courses, virtual and face-to-face instructor-led training, as well as a selection of FREE Business Analysis training.

Meanwhile, please enjoy this book. We appreciate any comments, suggestions, recommended improvements, or complaints that you care to share with us. You can reach us via email at eBooks@businessanalysisexperts.com.

INTRODUCTION TO
REQUIREMENTS ELICITATION TECHNIQUES

This chapter will help you:

- Understand why getting the right requirements for a proposed IT solution is so challenging

If everyone involved in defining a future Information Technology (IT) solution could express what he or she wants or needs the solution to deliver, you would not need this book. Of course, that implies that they would not need you as the one wearing the business analysis hat to help them discover their requirements. They could just jot them down and be done. Fortunately, for both you and us, that is not the real world.

Every analysis of IT projects over the past seventy-plus years identifies missing and misunderstood requirements as the major cause of project overruns and failures.

 Why is getting the right requirements for a proposed IT solution so challenging?

Several factors contribute to the challenge:

1. *Changing Business and Regulatory Environments*

IT applications are just one component of a complex business system that reacts to changes in the competitive business or regulatory environment. To meet the evolving needs of the business community, the underlying IT applications have to change. Due to the complexity of interactions between business systems that organizations need to survive, any change in one can trigger an avalanche of changes in other applications.

2. *The Evolution of Information Technology*

IT applications themselves evolve to take advantage of advances in the underlying technology and to keep up with evolving business needs. New versions of off-the-shelf software or new releases of homegrown applications are necessary to keep applications current, meaning change is a permanent fixture. Technology-based changes in one application often cause a ripple effect in downstream applications and can require changes to upstream applications as well. Recognizing and expressing the requirements for all impacted applications approaches the impossible.

3. *The Multitude of Stakeholders and Influencers Involved*

As business systems and IT applications increase in complexity, the number of people who influence how the business systems should change increases exponentially. Different people have different perceptions of how things work today and how they should work in the future. These competing interests and authorities often get in the way of effective communication on IT projects.

4. *The Fundamental Challenge of Human Communication*

Although we may share a common language, our understanding of it varies drastically. As human beings, we often have difficulty clearly expressing our intent in terms that guarantee a shared understanding with another person. Miscommunication increases when two people have diverging vocabularies like subject matter experts from different functional areas within an organization.

MANAGING REQUIREMENTS ELICITATION WITH A QUESTION FILE

This chapter will help you to:

- Create and use a structured question file to track what you know and what you do not know about the project at any point in time.

The process of doing business analysis is really about getting relevant requirements from all stakeholders. That takes time and one question that causes most people wearing the BA hat pain is, "How much longer are you going to take?" The obvious inference is that you have to get the requirements to the developers so they do the "real work" of creating the software to meet their deadline.

This chapter introduces a phenomenally simple technique that will give you a formula for answering that and similar questions with some degree of confidence. At the very least, you will be able to explain the rationale behind your answers.

A Question File Quantifies Uncertainty

Two of the biggest challenges for the one tasked with requirements elicitation for an IT project are,

"where to start?" and
"how do I know when I'm done?"

A simple concept we call the "Question File" is one of the best techniques we know for managing requirements elicitation. Its basis is uncertainty.

At the beginning of a project, you often have no idea what the project is supposed to deliver, who is involved, or how to get started. If you ask your manager, you may discover that you are not the only one who knows so little about the project — welcome to the Uncertainty Principle. If you happen to be knowledgeable about quantum physics, this name should sound familiar, but you may be surprised about our take on it. For normal people (i.e., all of us non-quantum-physicists), this definition of the uncertainty principle might even make sense.

To manage requirements elicitation, you need to leverage your uncertainty. The process of doing a project is actually one of reducing uncertainty - not eliminating it, unfortunately, because that is impossible. According to an old German saying, "Theory is when you know everything and nothing works. Reality is when everything works and you do not know why!"

Once you have your initial interview with the Project Sponsor, you have a general idea what the project will deliver. You probably feel relatively confident but the more you think about the interview, the more questions come to mind. Actually, you probably have a lot more questions after the interview than before it. As you continue to interview other stakeholders, your uncertainty grows because their answers are different than you expect.

As the project progresses and you interview more and more

stakeholders, there comes a time when their answers start to make sense within the context of the project based on your growing knowledge base.

Now you start to feel better because your uncertainty is dropping. You get the feeling that you might actually pull this thing off – and you just might if you can avoid the dreaded "analysis paralysis". So how can you use your uncertainty to recognize when it is time to quit asking questions (the hallmark of analysis) and document what the business community needs and wants in the form of requirements? In other words,

"when does requirements elicitation end?"

Discovering What You Do Not Know

Using a question file to manage requirements elicitation is an extremely simple yet powerful idea. If you think about it, all knowledge about a project falls into one of four basic categories at any point in time. Everything that you know about the project at that time belongs to a category we call the "Facts". Of course, there are different levels of facts and varying degrees of certainty about each fact. Nonetheless, we will stick with our original title for the sake of simplicity. More specifically, facts represent everything that you know you know about the project. That is an important distinction.

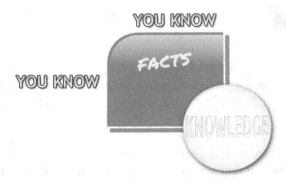

The next category represents things you know that you do not know about the project. Anytime you think of a question, you are actually discovering something that you know you do not know. If someone would give you an answer to your question, you would have a new fact. Of course, that assumes that the answer was from someone who has the knowledge to answer the question and the authority to ensure that his or her answer is the right one.

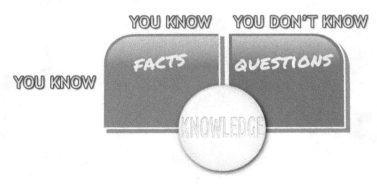

The next category contains things that you do not know that you do know (again, at any given point in time). How can you not know that you know something? Well, there are things you have done in the past on other projects or in past lives that will help you on your current project. You just have not identified them yet. We call that category "Experience".

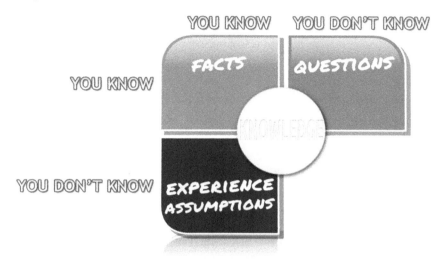

Something else belongs in this category as well, something we call "Assumptions". What happens if you cannot find anyone who has the authority and the knowledge to answer your questions? They may be unavailable for your project when you need the answer or maybe nobody has ever tried to do what you are trying to do (at least within your organization) so no one really knows the answer.

At some point, either someone will answer every open question or someone (the default being you) will make an assumption and act upon it. That is life, and we are not saying there is anything wrong with it per se. We are simply pointing out you need to recognize when you are making an assumption. If it is necessary, make the most likely assumption based on your experience and document it. Undocumented assumptions are the true project killers and managing requirements elicitation will help you eliminate them.

The fourth category contains things that you do not know you do not know (or, as some prefer to call it, 'the unknown unknowns"). We call it "Fate". Fate exists on every project, even the best run. There will always be things you do not know that you do not know, so you have no choice but to live with it. It is, however, the number of factors that fall into this category that will ultimately determine the success or failure of your project. For those who ignore this category, the word FATE often becomes an acronym for "Failure at the End"!

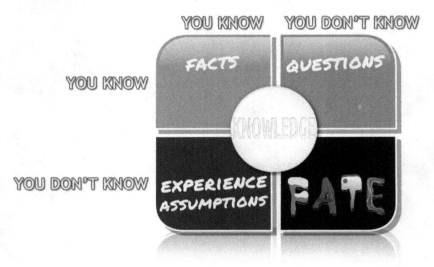

The challenge now has become, how can you manage requirements elicitation by tracking what *you know you know*, capturing what *you know you do not know*, and using what *you do not know you do know* to combat what *you do not know you do not know*? (If you can say that one three times without stuttering, that BA hat you are wearing should be a great fit!)

Minimal Layout of the Question File

Enter, the Question File. Simply put, the Question File is a repository for these four categories of knowledge (or lack thereof). It is one of the simplest forms of documentation for your project, but it just may be the most important document you create to avoid analysis paralysis.

So how do you structure an effective Question File? I recommend a simple spreadsheet with five columns. One column contains your questions expressed in a manner that any answer you get becomes a new fact. I do strongly recommend numbering and dating each question to keep track of when you recognized that you needed to know something. This step alone creates a great project history!

Date	Question
12/3	1 What is the average age of human beings in the wild?
12/5	2 Will manmade devices exceed the speed of light in our lifetime?
12/7	3 Is there intelligent life on other planets?
12/19	4 What's wrong with my golf swing?

The next column is the person amongst your stakeholders that you think has the knowledge and authority to answer the question. Identify this person by name or by job title and accept that your answer is subject to change as you learn more. You just think at this time that this person is your most likely source for getting the right answer. If he or she does not know the right answer, ask him or her who can. If he or she does not know, ask your manager, project sponsor, the janitor, the mail clerk, or anyone who might be able to guide you. Keep digging until you are confident that you have the answer from the person who has the appropriate knowledge and the authority.

Once you get an answer from the proper authority, document the response in the Answer column. In case you do not get an answer in time, make the best assumption you can to avoid delaying the project — but document that it is an assumption. Writing the word "ASSUMPTION:" in bold in front of whatever you assumed makes it easy to recognize. You might also consider color-coding the cell to make it stand out. Just make sure you document that this is an assumption and tell the world (or at least anyone who you think should have given you the answer) about your assumed answer.

Date		Question	Who	Answer
12/3	1	What is the average age of human beings in the wild?	Genome Project Leader	35 Years
12/5	2	Will manmade devices exceed the speed of light in our lifetime?	Arthur C. Clark	
12/7	3	Is there intelligent life on other planets?	???	**Assumption:** Yes, based on math
12/19	4	What's wrong with my golf swing?	Tiger Woods	

Consider a simple email that says something like,

"We need to know … and have not received a definitive answer to date. To avoid endangering our scheduled delivery date, as of MM/DD/YYYY we are working under the assumption that …. Please note that after that date, changes to that assumption must be submitted via a formal Change Request which may cause additional costs and/or shift the delivery date."

Give the recipient a reasonable amount of time to respond to your email. By the way, you will get much more mileage out of this approach if you avoid overusing it.

The final Date column is to document when you got the answer (or made the assumption).

Date		Question	Who	Answer	Date
12/3	1	What is the average age of human beings in the wild?	Genome Project Leader	35 Years	12/8
12/5	2	Will manmade devices exceed the speed of light in our lifetime?	Arthur C. Clark		
12/7	3	Is there intelligent life on other planets?	???	**Assumption:** *Yes, based on math*	12/31
12/19	4	What's wrong with my golf swing?	Tiger Woods		

Using a Question File
to Combat Analysis Paralysis

Now, if you had a Question File for your project, you could perform magic tricks.

For example, you could sort your file on the "Answer" column and count how many questions you had answered and how many were still open. The ratio of answered to open questions shows you the level of your uncertainty. If you followed our recommendation and inserted the word "ASSUMPTION:" in front of each assumed answer, you can also see the ratio of assumptions to answers from stakeholders.

Here is the secret: if you have very few questions in the file, you are probably very early in the project and you definitely need to dig deeper to get the answers you need.

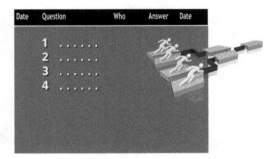

If you have many questions, most of which are unanswered, you are presumably in the midst of the analysis phase. It is too early to try to finalize the requirements; you need to keep going until you have more answers.

If you have a significant number of questions with answers AND you have been through a phase where the answers did not generate more questions than they resolved, you may be approaching the time to quit analyzing and start writing your requirements. It might even be time to finalize your requirements gathering efforts and close the remaining open questions with appropriate assumptions.

Date	Question	Who	Answer	Date
	1		......	
	2		......	
	3		......	
	4		......	
	5		Assumption	
	6		......	
	7		......	
	8		......	
	9		......	
	10		......	
	11		Assumption	
	12		......	
	13		......	
	14		......	

The ratios of Answered to Open questions and Answers to Assumptions are the best metrics for recognizing uncertainty and avoiding analysis paralysis. They are also a great metric for reporting to your manager how far along you are in your requirements gathering efforts.

You could also sort the file on the "Who" column to determine to whom you should be talking next. We recommend that you talk with the people who have the highest level of authority first and after that with those for whom you have the most questions. Getting information in descending order of authority makes it less likely to have answers overridden by a superior.

Another potential use of the Question File is to browse it comparing the date you identified the question with the date you got a response. The time difference between the two says something about the priority of the project from the perspective of the person identified in the "Who" column.

Finally, if someone new comes on to the project in the middle, the

Question File is invaluable as a tool for getting him or her up to speed quickly. You do not have to spend your time telling him or her everything that is in the file. As I said, magic tricks.

By the way, I generally seed my Question File with at least four questions:

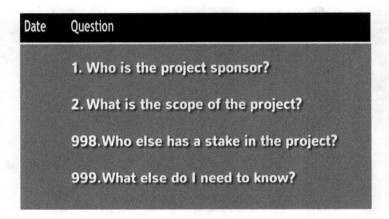

Date	Question
	1. Who is the project sponsor?
	2. What is the scope of the project?
	998. Who else has a stake in the project?
	999. What else do I need to know?

The first question reminds me of the first person I want to interview to get answers to the second and 998th questions. The second question reminds me to capture and manage what the project can and cannot do. Note the numbers of the final two questions in my initial list. They are set there on purpose to ensure that they stay at the end of the list. They keep me aware that there are things that I do not know I do not know. As the project progresses, I will repeatedly revisit those questions to try my best to manage FATE.

Online resources for you:

⇨ FREE Business Analysis Training
http://businessanalysisexperts.com/product-category/free-business-analysis-training/

⇨ 8 Probing Questions Every Business Analyst Should Ask
https://www.linkedin.com/pulse/8-probing-questions-every-business-analyst-should-ask-ron-phillips

⇨ The "What," "Who," and "Why" Questions of Business Analysis
http://www.dummies.com/how-to/content/the-147what148-147who148-and-147why148-questions-o.html

⇨ How to Ask All the Right Questions During Analysis
http://www.thebacoach.com/asking-all-the-right-questions/

Thomas and Angela Hathaway

IDENTIFYING STAKEHOLDERS FOR REQUIREMENTS DISCOVERY

This chapter will help you:

- Understand the consequences of missing stakeholders

- Identify all stakeholders of a project

A Stakeholder on an IT project is actually anyone who has the knowledge and the authority to affect the project or the solution. That obviously includes decision-makers and end-users. Beyond those obvious stakeholders, there can be a whole slew of other people within your organization that might have a say in what the delivered application and impacted business processes can or cannot do. Some of them may even come from outside your organization. Making sure you have identified all of them is an ongoing challenge.

Missing Stakeholders Means Missing Requirements

Imagine planning a "surprise" wedding without proposing to your bride-to-be. Imagine starting a project to remodel your house without consulting with your spouse. Imagine adding an additional floor to your house without consulting the local zoning authorities.

These three are but a few of the silly hypothetical scenarios that describe the real-life situations in which some organizations initiate information technology (IT) projects without including all relevant stakeholders. Involving the right decision makers is one of the critical success factors for any project, IT or otherwise.

To involve them, you have to first figure out who they are. Identifying stakeholders is one of the most important steps in the early phases of any project. Missing a single stakeholder might endanger the entire project. At the very least, discovering a missed stakeholder late in the project is a major contributing factor to scope creep. How can you avoid this pitfall?

We offer a proven set of hardcore techniques, methods, and tricks for identifying stakeholders and enabling them to discover their requirements. The more complete your list of stakeholders, the more likely you are to get a complete picture of what the business needs and what IT can contribute.

At the beginning of a new project, the first person you should talk to is the Project Sponsor. A Project Sponsor by any title is the person who has the authority to say what the project will or will not do — and the ability to fund the project. That person generally has the best idea of what he or she wants the project to achieve which makes him or her a great candidate for your first interview. Prepare yourself for that interview by jotting down the 5 – 9 high-level questions you need the Project Sponsor to answer.

At the end of that first interview, you typically recognize three things:

1.   The Project Sponsor's idea is a vision of the outcome of the project.

2.   That idea is probably big and no one (including the Project Sponsor) really knows how big.

3.   You have a lot more questions after the interview than before — your uncertainty is increasing.

Regardless what answers you get to your initial set of questions, capture them in some form (ideally electronic). If the Project Sponsor cannot answer one of your questions, ask her or him who in the organization can. In other words, who are all of the project's stakeholders and how can you identify them given just a vision statement?

Identifying Stakeholders on an Org Chart

The next place to look for stakeholders is a plain, old, simple org chart. Org charts tell you who is responsible for what within an organization. Unless they are electronic, they are notoriously susceptible to getting out-of-date. As a result, a lot of smaller organizations seldom maintain them. The good news is that they are very easy to create, so if your organization does not have one that is current, whip out your trusty org chart tool (e.g., a flipchart, white board, or any drawing software you might prefer) and throw one together. This is Agile Analysis at its best.

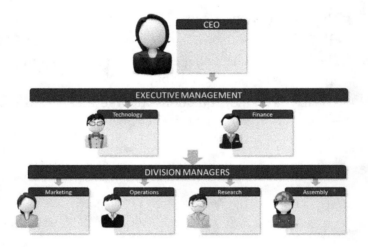

Once you have a reasonable facsimile of a current org chart, chat with your project sponsor (and perhaps your manager and peers) about whom on the org chart the project will affect. For starters, simply note on the chart which departments or units are "potentially involved parties". Eliminate only those units that the project will definitely not affect in any manner. If you are unsure, mark them as candidates. Remember, missing stakeholders cause missing requirements.

One group you might identify is a potentially large pool of participants who will be involved in actively creating the solution. Call this group of folks "Creators". This group might include analysts (i.e., yourself), designers, application architects, developers, testers (aka "software quality guardians"), managers, network administrators, system administrators, data base folks, and a whole slew of like-titled people who have a stake in your project. Ultimately, each of them might have a set of requirements that they can impose upon your project.

CREATORS

ANALYSTS (I.E., YOURSELF),
DESIGNERS,
APPLICATION ARCHITECTS,
DEVELOPERS,
TESTERS,
MANAGERS,
NETWORK ADMINISTRATORS,
SYSTEM ADMINISTRATORS,
DATA BASE FOLKS,
ETC.

The next group you should identify (arguably the most important group) we call "end users". The general idea behind developing a solution is that at some point in the future, real people in the real world will do real things with whatever your project delivers. Two potential pools of people you need to consider are the "Internal end users" and the "External end users".

Customer Service

Customer

Internal end users are people within your organization or at least within the project sponsor's sphere of influence. These are generally easier to get to than their external counterparts are. External end users could be Joe Blow and the Dixie Cups or anyone else on the planet (especially if you are developing software for the Internet). They can be exceedingly difficult to identify and more difficult to satisfy. For instance, if your project delivers a web app, you may have a thundering herd of external end users who will use your app in the future. How do you get their requirements?

Internal end users are your primary source for stakeholder requirements. They are ultimately responsible for representing the external end users' interests in the requirements gathering process. Since these are the people who will use the solution once it is developed, their responsibility (believe it or not) is to tell you before they have access to your solution what they want the thing to do, how they want it to look, what they need to know from it, and how they would prefer to interact with it.

Creating and Maintaining
a Stakeholder List

By now, you might recognize that there are many folks interested in your project. You might consider starting a list of everyone that you need to involve to get a good idea of what the project should deliver. You could even call this your "Stakeholder List".

No sooner do you start to chat with the identified stakeholders than you stumble across yet another group of folks who have something to say about what your solution must do, and that is the group we call "SIGs" or "Special Interests Groups". These might be methodology folks, a PMO (Project Management Office), the Legal Department, Auditors, Finance, Compliance, or any number of different areas within your organization.

SIGs have jurisdiction over something that your solution will affect or that will affect your application. Their responsibility is to express constraints based on their specific interests on what you can and cannot do, or more importantly, what your solution can and cannot do. These limits are constraining requirements that you need to discover before you can consider your requirements discovery activities complete.

OK, this is now sufficiently complicated that it deserves a recap. Starting with your project sponsor and a trusty org chart you whipped up for identifying stakeholders, you have discovered Creators, internal and external End Users, and SIGs.

You have added all of them to your Stakeholder List. Put that way, it sounds overly simple. The challenge is how to know that you have identified ALL of the relevant folks within each group.

Unfortunately, there is no single solution to solve this challenge. One idea is to share your stakeholder list whenever you interview a stakeholder. At the end of the interview, ask three final questions:

1. "Could this project affect anyone else that you can think of?"

2. "Is there anyone not on my Stakeholder List that could make a decision about the solution we create?"

3. "Could anyone that I have not identified care how the project is executed?"

If no one can add to your stakeholder list, your list is about as good as it is going to get. You probably will add to it when you analyze the business problems or create a process model (both of which are also excellent techniques for identifying stakeholders), but this technique gives you a great start.

Nevertheless, do not chisel your stakeholder list onto a stone tablet. A major component of managing change throughout the project is recognizing when changes to requirements changes who your project affects or who can affect your project. In addition, one of the often-overlooked causes of requirements change is personnel changes. Identifying stakeholders is a process that does not end until the project is finished.

Online resources for you:

⇨ Identifying and Analyzing Stakeholders and Their Interests
(Community Tool Box)
http://ctb.ku.edu/en/table-of-contents/participation/encouraging-involvement/identify-stakeholders/main

⇨ PMP Exam: Stakeholders
https://www.youtube.com/watch?v=R_7_nyj0ZQQ

⇨ Engaging Stakeholders for Project Success
https://www.pmi.org/~/media/PDF/learning/engaging-stakeholders-project-success.ashx

⇨ Stakeholder analysis for avoiding paralysis
http://ba-camp.org/wp-content/uploads/2014/05/Stakeholder-analysis-for-avoiding-paralysis-Ales-IIBA-Slo.pdf

⇨ BAwiki: Stakeholder Analysis
http://www.bawiki.com/wiki/concepts/stakeholders/stakeholder-analysis/

PROBLEM ANALYSIS
INITIATES REQUIREMENTS GATHERING

This chapter will help you:

- Define Problem Statements from all involved stakeholders

- Identify the "real" problem to focus requirements elicitation

Unless you as the one wearing the BA hat know what business problems your project will solve, you have little chance of figuring out whom to ask let alone what questions to ask. A well-expressed problem statement will justify your project and make the elicitation process run considerably smoother. As a final value add-on, it provides the ultimate test of your solution. The success of your project will be measured on whether and how well your solution solves the business problems. This section offers ideas on how to get to that well-expressed business problem statement.

Collect Problems from ALL Stakeholders

Understanding problems that the business community has with their current business systems is an essential component of gathering the requirements. An analysis of business problems identifies issues with software, user manuals, training, procedure documents, and much more. If you are working on a project and do not know what business problem the project will solve, you have no way of really knowing when you are done whether the project was successful or not. Worse, you have only limited ability while you are on the project to decide whether it is moving in the right direction or not.

Organizations that accept this premise generally have a place in their project initiation document called the "Problem Statements". Well-written Problem Statements focus all stakeholders, which facilitates and guides the requirements discovery process. As an added benefit, it also serves as a basis for end user acceptance testing. The challenge is how to get effective Problem Statements quickly. This challenge is non-trivial and requires a well-defined technique.

As a pre-requisite, let us assume that someone (presumably the project sponsor) defined the project scope in some manner. You need the project scope to get folks focused on what kinds of problems they should be identifying. Actually, the project sponsor might even be a great first person to ask what problem(s) this project will solve. By simply documenting the answers, you have initiated a Problem List! Do not attempt to analyze the sponsor's problems just yet; simply capture them.

Once you have your sponsor's answers, expand your Problem List by getting input from other stakeholders on the project. You might use email to solicit their business problems related to your project or, better yet, have a meeting (virtual or in person) in which the group can present their answers.

Ask each stakeholder, "what's wrong with the way things work today?". Your goal is to collect problems from the different perspectives of identified stakeholders.

We highly recommend the face-to-face (or if that is not possible, virtual) meeting over email because problem definition meetings:

⇨ give everyone involved an opportunity to hear other participants' problems

⇨ are a great team-building exercise

⇨ allow all attendees to actively read each other's body language

⇨ reveal additional "problems" feeding off of other stakeholders

⇨ provide ample opportunity for starting to identify potential solutions to the problems

On a side not, people will offer many solutions in the meeting that you called specifically to define problems. That is fine; do not ignore the solutions. Capture every presented idea. Under no circumstances, however, should you indicate or assume that the proposed solution might actually be what your project will deliver. It is much too early in the process for that. Many of the proposed solutions mighty show up later in your list of potential requirements for the project.

If you do not know what business problem your project is solving, you will never know when you are done. By initiating the project with a problem list you are setting the stage for success.

A Well-Structured Problem List

For each "problem" identified by a stakeholder:

1. Write it down as a complete sentence

You want to minimize ambiguity by expressing the problem in a simple, clear sentence. Get a concrete example or a clear definition so that everybody involved understands the problem as stated.

I have a problem with my mouse

I have a problem with my **COMPUTER** *mouse*

2. Get agreement with all involved parties that it is a problem from that stakeholder's perspective

Agreement leads to co-ownership of the problem, but sometimes getting agreement amongst a group of people is nearly impossible. Get at least one person to agree and then enlist that person to explain the issue to others. This process achieves consensus if not outright agreement.

If you cannot get agreement on a problem, put it on an "Open Issues" list. Be aware that anything on the Open Issues list represents a potential risk factor to your project until the issue is resolved. By the way, the Open Issues list is a wonderful by-product of the meeting.

3. Number the problem

You will make your life a whole lot simpler by having an identifier for each problem for future reference. Although you are numbering the problems sequentially as you discover them, the number becomes an identifier, meaning you should not change the number after the fact. Having a unique identifier for each captured problem will facilitate problem analysis and, later, relating business and stakeholder requirements back to the problems.

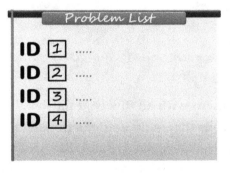

Now that you have an initial list of problems, use it to identify potentially missing stakeholders. For each problem on your list, ask:

4. Who else is interested in solving this problem?

The people most interested in solving this problem are probably the ones suffering from the effects. Other candidates are people or departments that could gain tangible or intangible benefits from a solution.

5. Who does not want the problem solved?

For some people in an organization, the problem represents an opportunity. Quite often, one group is experiencing a problem specifically because of how another group works. Including both perspectives in your analysis improves the probability of project success considerably.

6. Who can influence how we might solve this problem?

Projects inflict change and for every potential change in an organization, there are Special Interest Groups (SIGs — e.g., a Standards Committee, the Legal department, Compliance, Security, Audit – just to name a few). These are people who might not care about whether you solve the problem, but have the authority to limit what you can and cannot do.

Including the members of these groups will help you define most if not all relevant stakeholders for your project. That, in turn, will help you contain the ugly "Scope Creep Monster" in later stages of the project.

Missed stakeholders and undefined problems are major contributors to scope creep because you need to add new requirements to solve the additional business problems. Since you are involving a wide range of stakeholders from the start, the risk of eternally expanding requirements is much smaller.

On a side note, this approach will also lead to a more complete set of requirements because you are considering the needs of many different stakeholders from the beginning. It is an iterative process.

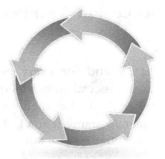

As soon as you identify new stakeholders in your project, find out what problems those stakeholders perceive. Repeat step 1, above to add the new problems to your original Problem List and continue numbering them sequentially. If new insights lead you to modify captured problems, make sure that everyone (not only the newly identified stakeholders) agrees with the modification.

Once you have a solid Problem List, you are ready to start

A Simple Problem Analysis Technique

Unless you do proper analysis, many Problem Statements sound more like "Solution Statements" because they describe what the project will deliver instead of what problem(s) it will solve. For example, "We need a new website" presupposes a solution; it is not a Problem Statement. "Website visitors cannot understand what we offer" expresses a problem that the proposed solution (a new website) could potentially solve.

Business Problem Analysis is a phenomenally simple but powerful technique for ensuring that your project is the right project and that it is delivering the right product. Our approach to Business Problem Analysis identifies the "Real" problem so you can formulate the Problem Statement. It adds context to the Problem Statement by identifying and grouping related symptoms. It seeds an initial list of potential requirement statements so that you do not have to start requirements discovery from scratch. Finally, the analyzed Problem Statements are a great input to requirements brainstorming.

Start with the list of problems that you gathered from all project stakeholders. Using it, your team of cross-functional stakeholders needs to make four fundamental decisions to identify the "Real" problem or problems.

1. Is It a Problem?

Does the problem express something that is wrong with the

current situation from one or more stakeholders' perspectives? Quite often in the process of creating a Problem List, items slip in although they are not really problems per se. They may be simple statements of fact, such as

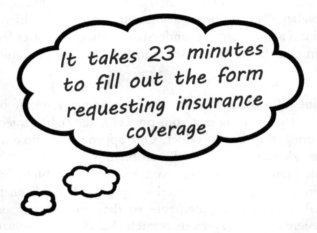

Is 23 minutes a problem or a speed record? You need to restate items like this to express a problem (i.e., "We are losing applicants because it takes 23 minutes to complete our on-line application form.") or remove the items from your list before you start. Otherwise, you will waste precious time debating and discussing them only to discover that many are irrelevant anyway.

By the way, we do not recommend deleting the items; you took the time to capture them, make good use of them. We suggest that you put those items that you remove on a list called "Irrelevant items". Distribute your list to your peers and managers to see if anyone else is interested in them.

2. Can You Solve It?

If the statement expresses a problem, can anyone on your team do anything about it? If no one on the team (including, by the way, the project sponsor) has the authority or means to do anything about the situation the statement describes, it is OUT OF SCOPE for your project even if it is a problem.

Move these statements to a separate list entitled, "Out of Scope Problems". Give this list to your manager or someone who can take charge of it. Maybe other projects are already involved in doing something about it and they might be grateful for your contributions.

3. Are There Multiple Solutions?

If the statement defines a problem, are there multiple potential solutions that are significantly different? By definition, a "Real" problem has multiple possible solutions. Quite often, when you ask people to tell you what problems they have with the current situation, they tell you what is missing, i.e. "We don't have a blog on our website." OK, assuming that it is a problem, how could you solve it? You could develop the blog in-house, outsource it, or buy one off-the-shelf. Each of these "solutions" expresses a different option on how to create the blog, but the outcome is the same. This statement is by this logic a solution in disguise.

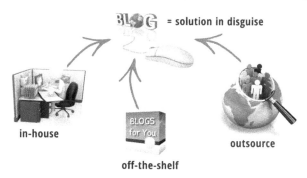

Not having a blog implies some negative consequences for the business, e.g., loss of traffic. Ergo the problem might be "We are losing traffic to dynamic websites that remain fresh by constantly posting new material on their blog." Note the shift from the solution (do not have a blog) to the problem (losing traffic). There are potentially many solutions to the problem of losing traffic and not all of them will result in adding a blog.

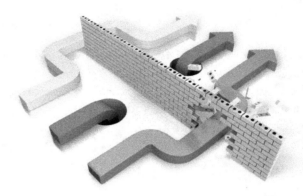

As a rule, any "problem" that states or implies something that is missing from the current situation is probably a solution or a requirement in disguise. Move it to a list titled "Possible Solutions / Requirements" to consider after you have isolated the "Real Problem". These might be valuable requirements or solutions, but they are not "the problem" your project needs to solve.

4. Is It a Symptom of a Different Problem?

For each remaining statement on the list, compare each item with every other statement and ask the question: "Assuming we could solve this problem, would any other 'problems' on the list 'go away'?" If the answer is yes, those "problems" are really symptoms.

Consider this analogy. You go to the doctor and tell her that you have back pain. For you, that is the "real" problem but your doctor sees it as a symptom of an underlying problem/disease.

If she tells you to take two aspirins and call her in the morning, she is masking the symptoms but not solving your problem. The problem will most likely return when you stop using the medicine. If she sends you to physical therapy or suggests surgery, she is trying to solve the "real" problem, meaning eliminate whatever causes your back pain. If the physical therapy or surgery solves the real problem, you will no longer have back pain.

In the business world, you as the one responsible for eliciting requirements are the doctor. You have to identify if a statement defines a "real" problem or is merely a symptom of an underlying problem. Make identified symptoms subordinate to the related problem to build a set. Once you are done with your entire list, you can evaluate each "real" problem together with its related symptoms. If you solve that real problem, all related symptoms disappear. If you cannot or decide not to solve the "real" problems but treat the symptoms instead, you should at least recognize that they could get worse over time.

 The item data base is out-of-date

 Warehouse is receiving orders with incorrect item numbers

Customers complain their invoices are incorrect

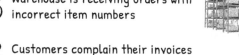

Will the Real Problem Please Stand Out

Based on my experience, a group, i.e. your team, is more efficient at this technique than any isolated individual is. To keep the momentum up, you need to go through the list once for each question.

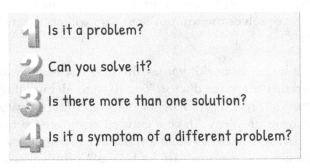

1. Is it a problem?
2. Can you solve it?
3. Is there more than one solution?
4. Is it a symptom of a different problem?

Attempting to answer all four questions for a single item leads to endless debate. It will actually take longer and deliver less reliable results. After each pass through your list, it is smaller as you will have removed some of the statements. The next step will then take less time. This is particularly important when you get to the fourth and final decision where you are really comparing each item on your list with every other remaining item. Your list has to be as small as possible to complete that final decision in a reasonable amount of time.

When you apply this technique in real life, you often find that one part of a problem goes away if you solve another problem, but a different part of the same problem does not. If that happens, split the Problem Statement in two, one that expresses the part that goes away (the symptom) and the other that expresses the unsolved remainder of the problem.

Group the symptom statement to the problem that solves it and add the unsolved remainder to the bottom of your "potential problem" list for later consideration.

This process eliminates everything that is out of scope, solutions disguised as problems, and symptoms of other problems. All of the statements left on your list must be "Real" problems. Simply stated, any statement that is a problem, is in scope for your project, is not a solution in disguise, and not a symptom of another problem is by definition a "REAL PROBLEM".

Review the real problems together with their related symptoms. You might need to wordsmith them a bit, but simply by grouping them into a set that describes the problem with all identified symptoms, you have come a long way toward achieving your goal of creating a well-expressed business Problem Statement.

As a byproduct of Business Problem Analysis, you created a list of potential solutions that might become requirements. You also have a set of well-expressed Problem Statements with associated symptoms that provide a phenomenal basis for testing any solution the project delivers. If you are trying to brainstorm requirements for an IT project that will solve business problems, schedule time to review the analyzed problem statements with the group immediately before you ask them to brainstorm solutions. Overall, those rewards make Business Problem Analysis one of the most effective tools for initiating requirements elicitation.

Online resources for you:

⇨ **View this chapter's content on YouTube**
Business Problems Drive Business Requirements (Part 1)
https://www.youtube.com/watch?v=bPcyjCk7kJ0
Problem Analysis Uncovers Business Requirements (Part 2)
https://www.youtube.com/watch?v=oLVlQdTudoI

⇨ Problem Analysis Techniques
https://www.miun.se/siteassets/fakulteter/nmt/summer-university/problemanalysispdf/

⇨ Defining and Analyzing the Problem
http://ctb.ku.edu/en/table-of-contents/analyze/analyze-community-problems-and-solutions/define-analyze-problem/main

⇨ Root Cause Analysis
Tracing a Problem to its Origins
https://www.mindtools.com/pages/article/newTMC_80.htm

⇨ 5 Whys: Root Cause Analysis and Problem Solving
https://www.youtube.com/watch?v=zAs40EbTPnw

⇨ Root Cause Analysis Examples
https://www.youtube.com/watch?v=IX3uQ72-iXs

REQUIREMENTS BRAINSTORMING

This chapter will help you:

- Prepare and conduct effective requirements brainstorming sessions to get initial requirements for an IT project.

No publication on techniques for eliciting requirements would be complete without a section on brainstorming. Unfortunately, many people think that brainstorming means getting a group of stakeholders together and asking them to "brainstorm" their requirements. If life were only that simple; unfortunately, successful brainstorming is hard work and this section is going to explain how you can achieve a successful brainstorming session.

To Brainstorm or Not to Brainstorm

Given the right setup, preparation, and rules, brainstorming is an extremely effective tool for expanding your list of potential requirements and generally speaking well worth the time investment.

Why is brainstorming so efficient at generating a ton of requirements? Well, people feed off each other's ideas. One person states an idea and everyone in the group hears it. That idea sparks another participant to express a related idea. The next person disagrees with a stated idea and throws out one that quantifies or negates it. If you eliminate discussion of other people's ideas (one of the core concepts of brainstorming), the only recourse people have is to offer alternatives.

Properly done, the outcome of requirements brainstorming can be impressive indeed. For example, in one 10-minute brainstorming session during a Requirements Gathering Workshop, a group of 20 participants identified 128 specific stakeholder requirements for a mission-critical application.

How can you achieve similar results on your project? For starters, you need an empowered, energized group of participants and you need to prepare them properly by getting them into the right mindset. Ideal participants are willing to think outside the box, share ideas even if they might sound stupid, and listen to other people's silly ideas. Discuss attitude with the group before you define the rules of engagement. Encourage them to let down their guards, disregard preconceived notions, and loosen up.

In our experience, the most productive groups have a ball during brainstorming. Stupid, even ridiculous ideas are just as prevalent as serious, well-thought-out ideas. Quite often, one member throws out a ludicrous idea just for laughs. Another member expands on that silly idea and the laughter gets louder. Suddenly, the silly idea sparks a brilliant solution that no one had previously considered and the group starts to generate a ton of specific, serious requirements that enable that brilliant solution. That is effective brainstorming at its finest.

If you are trying to brainstorm requirements for an IT project that will solve business problems, the participants need to understand the problems. Their participation in the business problem definition and analysis process is the preferred way to develop that awareness. If they did not develop the Problem Statements themselves, schedule time to review the analyzed problem statements with the group immediately before you ask them to brainstorm solutions.

To keep them focused, have the relevant problem statements prominently posted. The visibility of the problems allows people to scan the list while others are talking and develop potential requirements. Do not ask them to relate the idea to a specific problem, however, as that impedes the rapid exchange of ideas that underpins successful brainstorming.

Preparing the Session and the Participants

To prepare yourself for an effective requirements brainstorming session, you need:

- ☑ A countdown timer (there's an app for that — or use a stopwatch)

- ☑ Per participant, 3 Pass tokens (e.g., poker chips, playing cards, index cards with the word "Pass", tiny stuffed animals, etc.)

- ☑ Note pads and pens/pencils for each participant to doodle on or jot down ideas while awaiting their turn

- ☑ Legible, large-print lists of the problem statements with related symptoms to post on the walls of the room

- ☑ Legible, large-print list of your ground rules for effective brainstorming, e.g.:
    - Every idea is valuable
    - NO criticism of other people's ideas
    - NO discussion of presented ideas
    - NO inhibitions
    - Diversity of ideas is more important than details
    - You are looking for volume over quality

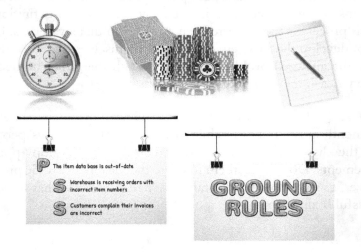

Once you have the right group of people with the right attitude in the right setting, describe the brainstorming process and present the visibly posted ground rules. Make sure that the group understands that you are looking for requirements not just for the software but also for the business solution of which the software is just one component.

⇨ Explain that requirements can be manual or automated functions, data, behaviors, or constraints that the solution has to exhibit when it goes live.

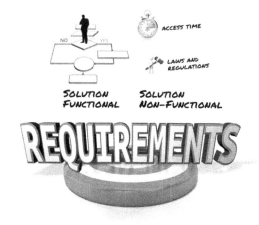

⇨ Give them specific examples of the types of requirements you want them to brainstorm.

⇨ Emphasize that the goal of the session is to generate as many potential requirements as possible in the allotted time.

⇨ Mention that the requirements should solve the posted problems but they could definitely go beyond that.

⇨ Encourage the group to let their eyes wander around the posted problems for ideas but not to limit their contributions to that list.

⇨ Remind them that they are defining the future but not to neglect whatever they want to keep from the current solution.

Set expectations by explaining that you will get them started by calling on each participant in turn. They should only speak when it is their turn. Each person will get 3 – 5 seconds to express the essence of a requirement in 3 – 5 words. Do not accept lengthy explanations of their requirement, just the essence of it. And, remember, each participant has three "Pass" tokens. They have to surrender one if they cannot voice a requirement in the allotted time. Once they run out of Pass tokens, you will not call on them in turn but they can still contribute an idea by raising their hand. They will have time to discuss and expand each idea after the brainstorming is over.

To avoid undue pressure on the first participant, we recommend a 15 - 30 second "get your mind in gear" pause before soliciting ideas. Set and communicate the time limit (typically 5 – 10 minutes) for the entire brainstorming session. Make sure everyone knows that the goal is volume of ideas, not depth of detail. Set the timer, pick a participant to start, and go.

Maintaining Momentum from Start to Finish

A limiting dimension of human behavior often interferes with active brainstorming, and that is that time passes more quickly for the facilitator than for the contributor. When calling on a person to contribute an idea, make sure to allow the full 3 – 5 seconds for an answer. Give him or her the time to formulate an idea by silently counting seconds ("1-Mississippi-2-Mississippi-3-Mississippi, or whatever …"). On the other hand, it is imperative to keep the session moving. If they do not have a response when the time is up, request his or her "Pass" token and move on.

Create and maintain a sense of urgency. Ask the first person to give you one requirement that the solution should satisfy and ask him or her to limit the answer to 3 – 5 words. Ask each participant in turn to either state a requirement or pass. Quite often, one person will "get on a roll" and want to throw out multiple requirements. Whereas you do not want to stifle the ideas, you have to avoid that person monopolizing the process to avoid other participants fading out.

In early iterations, ask each person to limit the response to one requirement at a time. Remind him or her that you will call on them again when it is their turn. After several participants have surrendered all of their allocated "Pass" tokens, you can be more liberal in allowing anyone on such a roll to express as many ideas as he or she desires.

When everyone is out of ideas and/or (more commonly) the time for the session is up, close it with a final question, "Can anyone think of anything they would like to add in closing?" Give the group at least seven seconds to answer. I recommend then asking each individual in turn directly if they have thought of anything they want to add.

Speed is essential to productive brainstorming. You need the synapses in the brains of the participants firing on all cylinders at top speed to minimize random thoughts that can stifle great ideas. To capture the flood of ideas that the group is contributing without impeding their pace, you need one non-participating note-taker per group of 3 – 5 participants.

The note-taker just captures the essence of each expressed idea and the initials of the contributor. To avoid slowing the group down, the note-taker should focus on capturing their ideas and not participate in idea generation. The note-taker should not speak to avoid interrupting the group.

Because non-participating note-takers add to the overhead of brainstorming, some facilitators prefer to record the session. Obviously, that requires a suitable device with sufficient audio quality to replay and understand every word the group utters. Imagine your frustration if you were to commit the time and effort to brainstorm brilliant ideas only to be asked later on to try to remember what you said because the recording was unintelligible. In addition, if you record their thoughts, it is often much more difficult to distribute the idea back to the original author for immediate expansion. Here again, time is critical and any significant delay between active brainstorming and expanding on the blurted out idea causes problems. Due to the hectic pace of life today, many people will not remember what the idea represented if you ask them a day or two later and that devalues the entire brainstorming concept.

Post-Session Steps and Lessons Learned

As soon as the 5 – 10 minute brainstorming session is over, distribute each captured idea back to the person who contributed it. Request that he or she convert the 3 – 5 word essence into a well-structured, complete statement that meets our criteria for effective requirements, meaning:

➪ It is a simple, complete, well-structured sentence

➪ It emphasizes WHAT the solution will do,
   Not HOW it will do it

➪ It is in scope for this project

➪ It is understandable, unambiguous, and clear
   to all target audiences

To prime your participants with the skill they need to write good requirements, consider teaching them in advance how to write effective requirements. You might recommend that they take our self-paced video course "Writing Requirements for IT — Simply Put!", before the session. If you work in an Agile Environment and are brainstorming User Stories, consider requiring the self-paced eCourse "Writing Effective User Stories". I have added the links to these courses in the "Online resources" at the end of this chapter.

You want each person to write the requirement that expands on his or her expressed idea. Minimize disturbances during this phase of the session by limiting discussions that might interrupt other people's thought process.

Make sure that the group knows before they start the brainstorming session that they will have this time to transform their captured ideas into legitimate requirements immediately after the brainstorming. This is actually a critical part of the brainstorming exercise. While they are transforming the ideas to become legitimate requirements, they can expand or modify the original thought.

Brainstormed Requirement

Maintain Warehouse reserves

Sentence Requirement

The store order cannot reduce the Warehouse on-hand quantity below the critical inventory (reserve) level for each item.

Encourage them to add any other related or non-related requirements that come to mind at that time. The overarching goal is to get a large set of potential requirements in the shortest amount of time possible. You will have time during requirements analysis to prioritize the requirements and eliminate any that are unnecessary.

- ☑ Getting the group into the right mindset primes the pump.

- ☑ Setting expectations by clearly explaining the process reduces anxiety and puts the group at ease.

- ☑ Visibly posting both the rules of engagement and the Problem List engages their visual sense while hearing other people's ideas engages the sense of hearing.

- ☑ Encouraging silly ideas reduces the tension and activates the subconscious where the best ideas originate.

- ☑ Having non-participant note-takers frees the group up to focus on the challenge of generating ideas without worrying about the idea getting lost.

The distinct separation between idea generation (brainstorming) and idea explanation (transforming the ideas into well-formed requirements) takes advantage of the latest research on how the human brain works. These two activities actually involve different parts of the brain that can interfere with each other. By allocating specific timeframes for each, you are minimizing the interference to produce more and better requirements.

To go back to the example I cited earlier, (the 20 participants brainstorming 128 requirements), although the active brainstorming component only lasted 10 minutes, it took the group 2 hours to complete the requirements. Take that into account when scheduling your brainstorming session. It is not just the time spent blurting out ideas.

Like everything else, people's ability to be productive in brainstorming sessions improves with practice. They have to be comfortable sharing their silly ideas with colleagues and peers without getting embarrassed. Many people have to get over that hurdle before they can fully contribute to the brainstorming outcome. Once they are there, however, brainstorming becomes an exhilarating experience that they can hardly wait to repeat.

One final word of caution, however. Effective brainstorming is extremely draining. The group cannot sustain productivity at that pace for too long or too often. Used prudently, however, brainstorming can easily become the most valued weapon in your arsenal of requirements elicitation techniques.

Online resources for you:

⇨ Writing Requirements for IT — Simply Put!
http://businessanalysisexperts.com/product/video-course-writing-requirements/

⇨ Writing Effective User Stories
http://businessanalysisexperts.com/product/video-course-writing-user-stories/

⇨ How To Brainstorm Like A Googler
http://www.fastcompany.com/3061059/your-most-productive-self/how-to-brainstorm-like-a-googler

⇨ Brainstorming: Generating Many Radical, Creative Ideas
https://www.mindtools.com/brainstm.html

⇨ In Pursuit of the Perfect Brainstorm
http://www.nytimes.com/2010/12/19/magazine/19Industry-t.html?_r=0

⇨ Using the Brainstorming Technique in Business Analysis
http://www.modernanalyst.com/Resources/Articles/tabid/115/ID/2067/Using-the-Brainstorming-Technique-in-Business-Analysis.aspx

⇨ 7 Techniques for More Effective Brainstorming
https://www.wrike.com/blog/techniques-effective-brainstorming/

⇨ How To Have Better Creative Thinking
https://www.youtube.com/watch?v=zO2LdDpx-Tc

⇨ Six Creative Ways To Brainstorm Ideas
https://www.youtube.com/watch?v=yAidvTKX6xM

TEN QUICK QUESTIONS
GUIDE REQUIREMENTS DISCOVERY

This chapter will help you:

- Adapt and use standard questions to initiate
  the requirements elicitation process
- Discover Functional and Non-functional requirements

Fundamentally, if someone gave you a list of all the questions you need to ask your stakeholders to get all of their requirements for your project, the creative component of business analysis would be done. Figuring out what to ask whom is the in our opinion the fun part; getting answers to the questions is mostly legwork. We promise not to give you all of the questions you need to ask. However, in this section we present a few time-honored, critical questions that you should at least consider to see if they are relevant for your project. If you do not ask these questions, you run the risk of missing critical requirements. We call them the Quick 10.

Introduction to the Quick Ten

Preparing questions for which you need answers on a given project is critical to the success of your requirements interviews. The one wearing the BA hat needs to use his or her natural curiosity to figure out what questions to ask. Organize those questions into a list or question file for quick access and update the list anytime a new question arises.

Because every project is unique, every organization is unique, and every SME is unique, it is impossible to know exactly what questions you should ask in your situation. Nonetheless, after many years of trial and error we have collected a set of what we consider critical questions for just about any type of IT project. These questions may not be universally applicable, but they serve as a great starting point.

We maintain that if you have not considered all ten questions, you are probably missing requirements. We call the list the "Quick 10" because we think you should try to get the first-cut (high-level) answers to these ten questions within the first thirty minutes of your project. The questions are recursive, meaning you can ask them repeatedly throughout the project at ever-increasing levels of detail. At the beginning of the project, you are looking for very high-level answers. Typically, this would be during an interview of a senior executive, your project sponsor, or your manager.

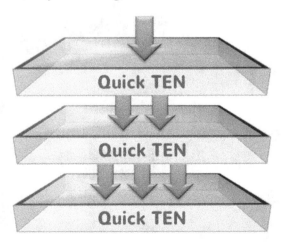

As the project proceeds, you can drill down in detail by asking the same questions repeatedly of the various stakeholders on the project to get more and more detailed responses. After taking our instructor-led training, many organizations seed their Question File with their own adaptation of these critical questions.

So what are these critical ten questions? We will present the questions and offer examples of their use based on an initial interview with the project sponsor of a fictional "Cash Forecaster" project that will predict the account balances for all bank and credit card accounts for her company.

OK

Discovering Functional Requirements

The first thing you need to know about any IT solution is, "What will it do when it is delivered"? You are trying to identify the primary **FUNCTION** that the application will perform.

Software always does something; if it does not do anything, it is not software. In other words, you need to identify the primary purpose of the application. When we posed this question to our Project Sponsor, she responded,

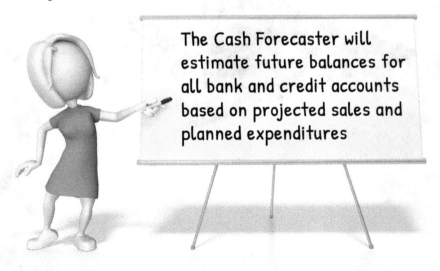

The Cash Forecaster will estimate future balances for all bank and credit accounts based on projected sales and planned expenditures

Since business applications generally exist to process information, another way of asking what the primary function is might be to approach it from the data side. Creating output is generally the application's primary function. When we asked the Project Sponsor what data the application would produce, she replied,

It will provide projected weekly account balances for all active bank accounts and credit cards for 18 months into the future

We captured her responses verbatim in our Quick Ten form:

QUICK TEN

Function	What will the function (process) accomplish (in a single sentence)? What information (results) will it generate?
Example *for the "Cash Forecaster"*	"The Cash Forecaster will estimate future account balances for all bank and credit card accounts based on projected sales and planned expenditures. It will provide projected weekly account balances for all active bank accounts and credit cards for 18 months into the future."

The second question to ask is what **INFORMATION** will the application need to do its job? This addresses the data input dimension. Where does the needed data originate?

Every function (including the primary function) needs data to do its job. At the beginning of the project, you cannot expect to get low-level details for every single element of data that the application will manipulate, like Account-ID, Credit-Card-Issuer, etc. Do not worry; you will get to that level of detail much later. If you drill down too far too soon, you risk missing the big picture perspective and can easily overlook critical data components. At the beginning of a project, you just need to know what general types or categories of data will be involved.

We asked our Project Sponsor, "What types of data does the Cash Forecaster need to be able to estimate the future balances?" She lists several off the top of her head and we capture her response in this example:

QUICK TEN

Information	What data does the application need and where is it?
Example *for the "Cash Forecaster"*	"Bank account balances and transactions, credit card balances and transactions, projected sales figures, fixed expenditures, and sales-dependent expenditures like delivery costs and taxes. They all come from Accounting; Sales projections come from the Director of Sales and Marketing; planned expenditures have to be approved by the appropriate executive for each division."

Obviously, this list is incomplete. As our analysis progresses, we will identify other data that the Project Sponsor did not list. That is a natural function of analysis, so do not be too concerned about ensuring that your list is complete at this time. Consider your Project Sponsor's answer a preliminary list.

These first two questions define the functional requirements at the appropriate level of detail, namely what the application will do (Forecast Account Balances), its input (Financial projections), and its output (Projected Cash-on-hand). We will show you a more detailed example later. Right now, we are off to a great start!

Getting Non-Functional Requirements

We designed the next four questions primarily to drive out common Non-Functional Requirements (NFR).

QUICK TEN

Frequency	
Urgency	
Volume	
Accuracy	

The **FREQUENCY** question deals with the volume of events that the defined function will have to deal with over a specified timeframe. The question to ask is, "How often will this function or application be used?" Beyond frequency of usage, you need to know whether the usage is cyclic (i.e. always follows a set pattern) or ad hoc (no discernable pattern).

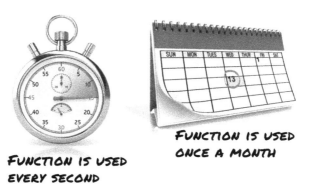

FUNCTION IS USED
EVERY SECOND

FUNCTION IS USED
ONCE A MONTH

By the way, when you are asking the Frequency question, do not limit it to human interaction. In today's wired world, many applications use other applications without human involvement. For instance, Ecommerce websites might use a web app that provides up-to-the-minute credit scores hundreds, thousands, or even millions of times per minute. In addition, there may be hourly, daily, weekly, monthly, and annual peaks (for example, Christmas Season).

UPDATES X TIMES
PER MINUTE

The answer to the frequency question gives developers insight into how much effort they need to invest to ensure that the application can meet projected demands.

QUICK TEN

Frequency	How often will the function be used? Is it Cyclic vs. Ad Hoc (peak time and volume)?
Example *for the "Cash Forecaster"*	"We need weekly updates to keep the projections relatively current. Its use by company executives will fluctuate depending on how tight money is at any point in time. In good times, they will probably only look at the forecast once a month, sometimes only once a quarter. When cash gets tight, they may need access weekly or any time there is a significant change to our cash flow."

The **URGENCY** question is of high interest for any application that involves interaction, again whether it is with people or with other applications. When users are waiting on a response from your application, the real question is, "How long can a user wait on a response from my function before he, she, or it can no longer do their job?" We call this the **Response Urgency**.

The question for the Cash Forecaster is, "How long can an executive wait on a request for a forecasted account balance?" Since the executive might need the information to make a quick decision, our Project Sponsor's response is, "One or two seconds."

The corollary from your application side is, "How long can your application or function wait on input from an outside source (i.e., a user or another application) before your application fails?" That is its **Update Urgency**.

QUICK TEN

Urgency	How long can a user wait on information (Response time)? How long can the application wait on information (Update Urgency)?
Example *for the "Cash Forecaster"*	"1 – 2 seconds" "Start of the first business day of the following week."

The **VOLUME** question deals with data. What you really need to know at the beginning of the project is just an order-of-magnitude. Will the application track hundreds, thousands, or millions of things? If you are creating a report, you need to know about how long the report is going to be, i.e. how many pages of printed material or how long could a web page get. If you are dealing with a web ordering system, you might ask how many items could be on the largest order possible.

When asking about volumes, it is important to project potential growth patterns. Is it possible that the volume of data will change significantly over the life of the application? If you were dealing with an order processing application, you would hope that the number of customers your application tracks would grow consistently over time so plan for future expansion.

QUICK TEN

Volume	For each output, how much information in business terms (pages, screens, windows, etc.) are you producing?
Example *for the "Cash Forecaster"*	"Less than 10 bank accounts and up to 50 credit card accounts. No significant growth is expected."

The **ACCURACY** question also deals with data. What you really need to know is, "What degree of error in the data would be acceptable to the business community?" If you ask a Subject Matter Expert this question, most would answer, "The data has to be 100% accurate, of course." The problem with that answer is that it is impossible to achieve.

The real question you should ask is, "How precise does the information have to be?" Precision is the number of decimal places the application will have to manage for numeric data. Our Cash Forecaster Project Sponsor is only interested in data that is accurate to the nearest 1000 dollars for each account. Typical accounting applications, on the other hand, commonly need data accurate to the penny (two decimal places). Some forecasting applications for large organizations might need to be accurate to the nearest million dollars.

Beyond precision, another dimension of accuracy is how current accurate data has to be. What risk does out-of-date information pose? You need to know how long the application can wait before it updates the information to reflect changes in the real world.

QUICK TEN

Accuracy	How precise does the data have to be?
	How current does it have to be?
Example *for the "Cash Forecaster"*	"Precise to the nearest $1000 per account"
	"As of close of business on the last business day of the previous week."

Capturing Constraints

The final questions in our list of critical questions deal with a category we call "Constraints". In our terminology, a constraint is an absolute limitation that nobody on the project team has the ability or the authority to affect in any manner. Some constraints are external (imposed by the world around us) while others are internal (imposed by other groups within our organization), but all constraints impose absolute limits on the solution.

BUSINESS POLICIES AND BUSINESS RULES are internal constraints. People within your organization have the authority to express business rules and change business policies but those people are typically external to your project. They define how your organization behaves independent of automation. For example, your organization might have a business rule that allows a discount to veterans or any other select group of customers. Business policies and rules often apply to all relevant applications (for example, online sales, direct sales, affiliate sales, etc.). They are not just for your project.

In today's data-dependent, hacker-vulnerable world, access to applications and data is a major concern. Therefore, a common example of business rules and policies deals with managing and enforcing application security.

QUICK TEN

Rules and Policies	What business rules or policies (e.g., security, authority, organizational structure, etc.) affect the project?
Example *for the "Cash Forecaster"*	"Business Rule: Access to the forecast is limited to Division Managers and above." "Business Policy: The CFO (Chief Financial Officer) will review and approve all updates to the Cash Forecaster." "Business Rule: Truncate projected account balances to the nearest $1000."

PEOPLE who will interact with your future application pose their own category of constraints based on their background and abilities. You need to know a lot about all different user groups who will be interacting with the function or application you are defining. Some common questions you need to ask are:

⇨ How comfortable are they with the technology?

⇨ What do they expect to achieve when they use the application or function?

⇨ What is their background?

⇨ What language(s) do they understand (not just native languages like English, French, and German but also domain languages — for example, sales, finances, technology, legal, etc.)?

⇨ What kind of turnover do you anticipate in the user groups (low, medium, or high)? Applications serving a high turnover group typically need additional support such as an interactive tutorial for getting new users up to speed quickly. Those with lower turnover might only require up-front training to familiarize a new user with the functionality of the application or function.

⇨ What is their culture (national culture as well as corporate culture)?

Consider what skills the users of the application need to use it effectively. Also, consider anything that you can think of that could potentially limit an individual's ability to interact with your application or function. All of those are potential People-related constraints.

QUICK TEN

People	What are the relevant user characteristics (roles, skills, desired experience, physical location, training, culture, etc.)?
Example *for the "Cash Forecaster"*	"The primary users are the executives. They should be comfortable with the technology since it is their phones or tablets. They are expecting a reliable forecast so they can make adjustments or investment decisions. They understand common financial terms in English. Turnover is light at that level so we should not spend an inordinate amount on a fancy built-in help facility. An hour or so of up-front training should suffice. Right now, they are all US citizens and we expect to keep it that way."

ENVIRONMENTAL CONSTRAINTS are limits imposed by the physical environment in which the application or function will exist. We are talking about things like the speed of light, external temperatures, time of day, etc.

Nobody can change those absolute values but unless you define all that are relevant, your application can and probably will fail.

A subset of Environmental Constraints is **INFRASTRUCTURE CONSTRAINTS**. They involve things like high-speed Internet access, an uninterrupted power supply, installed hardware and software platforms, etc. There are people within your organization who can change these (meaning they are technically internal), but they are generally outside the authority of the project team – which makes this category of constraints external by definition.

Your job as the one wearing the BA hat is to identify and express any relevant environmental and infrastructure constraints as requirements.

QUICK TEN

Environmental and Infrastructure	What Environmental limits does the location where the function / application will be used impose? What Infrastructure limits does the location where the function / application will be used impose?
Example *for the "Cash Forecaster"*	"N/A." "It has to run on the existing hardware and software platform. It also has to be accessible from authorized smart phones and / or tablets."

LAWS AND REGULATIONS are very commonly neglected external constraints. If you are defining the requirements for an application that has to deal with patient data, you have to be familiar with the Health Insurance Portability and Accountability Act (HIPAA). The Americans with Disabilities Act (ADA) is a universal example of restrictions imposed upon software that large audiences use.

This category of constraints becomes even more complex when you distribute your application to a global audience due to the added complexity of multiple governments.

At the current time, the rapid evolution of the IT industry has created a situation in which lawmakers and regulators around the world are struggling to keep up. You can expect a growing number of laws and regulations in the upcoming years to limit what you can and cannot do with software, meaning this category is likely to get much, much larger in the future.

Discovering and understanding regulatory constraints often involves interviewing someone from a Legal or Compliance Department within your organization.

QUICK TEN

Laws and Regulations	What laws, regulations, or external constraints affect the function?
Example *for the "Cash Forecaster"*	"N/A."

Using the Quick Ten

Those are the critical "Quick Ten" questions. As mentioned earlier, you should try to get the first cut at the answers to those 10 questions within the first 30 minutes of your project. You might actually want to go to your initial interview with the Project Sponsor with these questions prepared. You can adapt the terminology to fit your situation. We mentioned that these questions are reusable, meaning you can ask the same 10 questions at every appropriate level of detail.

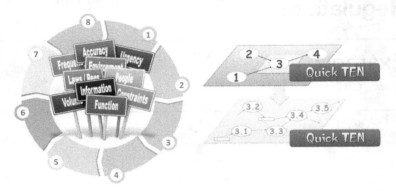

For example, a quick analysis of the information the Project Sponsor provided indicates that you should probably interview the Director of Budgeting and the Director of Sales and Marketing to get their requirements next.

The following table shows the Quick Ten questions adapted to the next level of detail with the answers from the Director of Sales and Marketing regarding the Sales Projector function.

QUICK TEN

Function	The Cash Forecaster Application (CFA) needs sales projections. What exactly will the Sales Projector do? What information (results) will it generate?
Example *for the "Cash Forecaster"* *(Project Item Sales)*	The Sales Projector will predict future product sales based on item sales history adjusted for seasonality and the potential impact of marketing campaigns. It will produce estimated weekly Item Sales by department for the following 18 months.
Information	What data does the function need and where is it?
Example *for the "Cash Forecaster"* *(Project Item Sales)*	The Sales Projector needs Item Sales by department from the past 7 years, which we get from the Sales History Data Warehouse.
Frequency	How often will the function be used? Is it Cyclic vs. Ad Hoc (peak time and volume)?
Example *for the "Cash Forecaster"* *(Project Item Sales)*	Department managers will use the function once a week to guess how many of each item they think will sell in the following week.

Urgency	How long can a user wait on information (Response time)? How long can the application wait on information (Update Urgency)?
Example *for the "Cash Forecaster"* *(Project Item Sales)*	1 – 2 seconds We have to project sales weekly with sufficient lead-time to order replacement items from our suppliers.
Volumes	For each output, how much information in business terms (pages, windows, etc.) are you producing?
Example *for the "Cash Forecaster"* *(Project Item Sales)*	We sell 50 – 100 different items right now but expect to be offering double that within a year.
Accuracy	How precise does the data have to be? How current does it have to be?
Example *for the "Cash Forecaster"* *(Project Item Sales)*	Within 10% of actual sales per item is our target. We are generally pretty close to that. We need to base our predictions on the sales as of close of business Wednesday for each week.

Rules and Policies	What business rules or policies affect the project (security, authority, organizational structure, etc.)?
Example *for the "Cash Forecaster"* *(Project Item Sales)*	The application will enforce corporate security standards controlling and monitoring its usage.
People	What are the relevant user characteristics (roles, skills, desired experience, physical location, training, culture, etc.)?
Example *for the "Cash Forecaster"* *(Project Item Sales)*	The primary users are the department managers. They are comfortable with the technology since it is their phones or tablets. They need access to the historical sales data and any scheduled events that might affect future sales of any item in their department. They will use the application while walking around in their department. We have a relatively stable workforce, so we do not have a high turnover here. I think a one-day training program should be enough to cover all department managers in the use of the new system.

Environmental and Infrastructure	What limits does the location where the function will be performed impose (space, size, speed)? Run on the existing hardware and software platform Accessible from authorized smart phones and/or tablets
Example *for the "Cash Forecaster" (Project Item Sales)*	Run on the existing hardware and software platform Accessible from authorized smart phones and/or tablets
Laws / Regulations	What laws, regulations, or external constraints affect the function?
Example *for the "Cash Forecaster" (Project Item Sales)*	N/A

Quite often, you will discover discrepancies between the answers at this level of detail and those at the higher level. That indicates an area you need to investigate further to clarify the source of the discrepancies and analyze the impact that might have on your project.

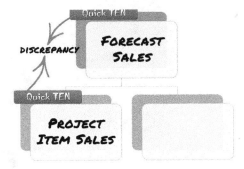

Until you have asked each of the 10 questions of the responsible SME for every functional and informational component of the application, you risk missing specific, non-functional requirements. Given the complexity of modern applications, that can lead you to a thundering herd of questions.

Online resources for you:

⇨ Exposing Functional AND Non-Functional Requirements
http://businessanalysisexperts.com/product/video-course-exposing-functional-and-non-functional-requirements/

⇨ Smart.BA – Non-functional requirements
http://www.smart-ba.com/articles/Non%20functional%20requirements.pdf

⇨ Organizational Requirements Engineering: Non-functional Requirements
http://www.iai.uni-bonn.de/III/lehre/vorlesungen/SWT/RE05/slides/09_Non-functional%20Requirements.pdf

⇨ Non-Functional Requirements, University of Ottawa
http://www.site.uottawa.ca/~bochmann/SEG3101/Notes/SEG3101-ch3-4%20-%20Non-Functional%20Requirements%20-%20Qualities.pdf

⇨ Use Cases and Functional Requirements
https://www.youtube.com/watch?v=HshfGCgWaE4

⇨ What Is a Use Case
https://www.youtube.com/watch?v=nN7ITDWKP6g

⇨ What Goes Into a Functional Specification?
http://www.bridging-the-gap.com/functional-specification/

REQUIREMENTS ELICITATION TECHNIQUES WRAP-UP

This chapter will help you:

- Review the contents of the book

- Prepare a plan for implementing new concepts

In this book, we presented specific techniques for eliciting requirements from subject matter experts (SMEs). We started with a simple approach for identifying stakeholders and creating a stakeholder list because missing stakeholders is one of the primary contributors to missed and misunderstood requirements leading to late project scope creep and overruns.

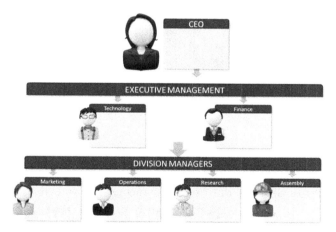

We introduced the Question File as a tool for managing the requirements elicitation process. We gave you the ability to track progress based on the number of open questions, percentage of answered questions, percentage of assumptions to answers, etc.

Date	Question	Who	Answer	Date
12/3	What is the average age of human beings in the wild?	Genome Project Leader	35 Years	12/8
12/5	Will manmade devices exceed the speed of light in our lifetime?	Arthur C. Clark		
12/7	Is there intelligent life on other planets?	???		
12/19	What's wrong with my golf swing?	Tiger Woods		

In our personal experience, the ability to report completion statistics like these for the elicitation process can do more to relieve the stress for the one wearing the BA hat than any other single technique we know.

Our approach to business problem definition and analysis will help you create a problem statement that sells a project based on its merits and allows executives to make informed decisions on project priorities.

☑ It identifies the real business problem(s) and justifies the business case for the project.

☑ It minimizes the time and money wasted on projects that simply fix symptoms and ensures that your limited resources are spent fixing "real" problems.

☑ As a side-effect, it lets you identify non-obvious stakeholders early in the project while giving all project stakeholders a much clearer picture of what the project is ultimately going to do and why.

☑ It also gives you a leg up on initial requirements definition, a step that many people find extremely challenging.

☑ Finally, it significantly reduces the risk of missing and misunderstood requirements and gives you a baseline for testing the success of the entire project.

If the identified business problems disappear when the project is complete, the project will have been successful.

We have applied the requirements brainstorming method we described in hundreds of projects over the years (both IT projects and personal projects).

☑ It never ceases to amaze our customers how effective this approach is for discovering hidden requirements.

☑ It increases the awareness of the sheer size of the project during the analysis phase when it is relatively cheap to rethink business decisions.

☑ On some projects, this awareness led to the justified cancellation of a project that would otherwise have failed much later and much more expensively.

☑ For other projects, it enabled the delivery of a complete business solution in weeks instead of months or years.

The Quick 10 questions are an adaptation of a list that Dan Myers originally introduced us to many years ago. We have personally experienced how painful it can be for IT projects that neglect any of the presented dimensions to requirements.

These questions are not "cast in concrete" and may need significant tweaking to fit your situation. However, the general idea of having a common set of questions like these for project initiation helps set a standard for all projects and that makes resource sharing across projects much simpler.

What Do You Do Next?

We do not pretend that this publication covers every possible requirements elicitation technique. Our focus has been on presenting techniques that we have used hundreds of times in our business analysis careers and that we have not seen published elsewhere. We trust that these techniques will help you improve the odds of defining working IT solutions that will meet your customers' needs.

In closing, we would like to offer a popular technique from our instructor-led classes that will help you implement the ideas presented in this book. We based this idea on the recognition that learning is a process, not an event. Few people can implement a new way of thinking and working based solely on what they learned in a course or from a book. According to current learning theory, we learn truly by doing. To get you started on that path, we suggest creating a plan (admittedly a novel idea!).

Simply jot down the name of the technique (you can use what we called the technique or create a more memorable name of your own).

Write down a reference to the lecture or page in the course or book where we presented the technique. Try to identify the situation and date when you expect to have an opportunity to try the technique out and, if you have the luxury, identify who within your group might be able to assist you. Just before you try that technique out, you might want to review the relevant chapter or section.

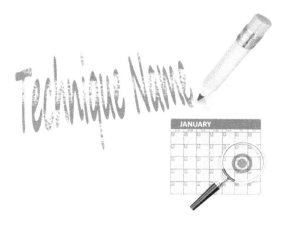

If it works as-is, that is fantastic! If it does not work or does not deliver the results you need, review that section of the publication again to see if you missed anything. If you think that you did everything right, feel free to contact us or to change the technique, adapt it, and make it work for you. Learning is about changing your behavior to acquire new abilities and that often means adapting a new technique to your view of the world.

In addition, we appreciate any feedback you have on your experience. Shared knowledge increases exponentially, and we will continue to share our insights or epiphanies regarding how to best get the right requirements from the right people at the right time to make your IT projects succeed. If you would like to contribute your feedback and experience, email Tom.Hathaway@ba-experts.com and we will acknowledge your contributions in our future publications.

Do not forget, missing and misunderstood requirements are still the Number one cause of IT project failure and have been since we invented these things called computers. Anything you can do to reduce the risk of that happening to your projects will greatly enhance the probability of your personal and professional success.

Online resources for you:

⇨ What Exactly Is Requirements Elicitation
  https://www.youtube.com/watch?v=vSXn16qMEZo

⇨ An Overview of Requirements Elicitation
  http://www.modernanalyst.com/Resources/Articles/tabid/115/ID/1427/An-Overview-of-Requirements-Elicitation.aspx

⇨ The Top 8 Mistakes In Requirements Elicitation
  https://www.batimes.com/articles/the-top-8-mistakes-in-requirements-elicitation.html

⇨ Are IT Requirements Elicited, Gathered, Captured, Defined or …?
  http://businessanalysisexperts.com/it-requirements-elicitation-stakeholder/

⇨ Make Requirements Discovery Easy With Checklists That Cover Every Important Question to Ask
  http://www.bridging-the-gap.com/requirements-checklist-pack/

⇨ Introduction to Requirements Elicitation Interviews & Workshops
  https://www.youtube.com/watch?v=e5Ci4XBCr4A

⇨ Requirements Elicitation Interviews and Workshops – Simply Put! - Best Practices, Skills, and Attitudes for Requirements Gathering on IT Projects
  http://businessanalysisexperts.com/product/ebook-requirements-elicitation-interviews-workshops/

⇨ Agile Requirements Elicitation
  http://agile.csc.ncsu.edu/SEMaterials/AgileRE.pdf

⇨ Business Analysis Guidebook/Facilitation and Elicitation Techniques
  https://en.wikibooks.org/wiki/Business_Analysis_Guidebook/Facilitation_and_Elicitation_Techniques

⇨ BABOK: 1.6 Techniques
http://www.iiba.org/babok-guide/babok-guide-v2/babok-guide-online/chapter-one-introduction/1-6-techniques.aspx

⇨ Requirements Elicitation: A Survey of Techniques, Approaches, and Tools
https://opus.lib.uts.edu.au/bitstream/10453/11626/1/2005003295.pdf

⇨ Assessment of Requirement Elicitation Tools and Techniques by Various Parameters
http://article.sciencepublishinggroup.com/pdf/10.11648.j.se.20150302.11.pdf

⇨ What Questions Do I Ask During Requirements Elicitation?
http://www.bridging-the-gap.com/what-questions-do-i-ask-during-requirements-elicitation/

⇨ Comparison of Various Requirements Elicitation Techniques
http://research.ijcaonline.org/volume116/number4/pxc3902408.pdf

⇨ 9 ways front-loading requirements can reduce enterprise software risk
http://www.cio.com/article/2935636/enterprise-software/9-ways-front-loading-requirements-development-reduces-enterprise-software-risks.html

⇨ The benefits of doing a detailed enterprise software requirements analysis
http://www.cio.com/article/2923225/enterprise-software/the-benefits-of-doing-a-detailed-requirements-analysis-before-selecting-enterprise-software.html

⇨ Projects Without Borders: Gathering Requirements on a Multicultural Project
http://www.computerworld.com/article/2562856/it-management/projects-without-borders--gathering-requirements-on-a-multicultural-project.html

ABOUT THE AUTHORS

Angela and Tom Hathaway have authored and delivered hundreds of training courses and publications for business analysts around the world. They have facilitated hundreds of requirements discovery sessions for information technology projects under a variety of acronyms (JAD, ASAP, JADr, JRP, etc.). Based on their personal journey and experiences reported by their students, they recognized how much anyone can benefit from improving their requirements elicitation skills.

Angela's and Tom's mission is to allow anyone, anywhere access to simple, easy-to-learn business analysis techniques by sharing their experience and expertise in their business analysis training seminars, blogs, books, and public presentations.

At BA-EXPERTS (http://businessanalysisexperts.com/) we focus exclusively on Business Analysis for **"anyone wearing the BA hat™"**. We believe that business analysis has become a needed skill for every business professional whether or not they have the title Business Analyst. We have made it our goal to enable anyone wearing the BA hat™ to have access to high quality training material and performance support. Please call us at 702-637-4573, email us (Tom.Hathaway@ba-experts.com), or visit our Business Analyst Learning Store at (http://businessanalysisexperts.com/business-analysis-training-store/) if you are interested in other training offers. Amongst other offers, the content of this book is also available as an eCourse on our website.

www.ingramcontent.com/pod-product-compliance
Lightning Source LLC
Chambersburg PA
CBHW060943050326
40689CB00012B/2557